Montessori Classroom Lesson Plans:

March

Spring/Asia/Amphibians and Reptiles

By

Robin Norgren, M.A.

"There is a great sense of community within the Montessori classroom, where children of differing ages work together in an atmosphere of cooperation rather than competitiveness. There is respect for the environment and for the individuals within it, which comes through experience of freedom within the community."

~ Maria Montessori

info@brightchildmontessori.com

The curriculum is dedicated to my children Jerry and Josey who were my first teachers of the joy found in following a child.

""The essence of independence is to be able to do something for one's self. Adults work to finish a task, but the child works in order to grow, and is working to create the adult, the person that is to be. Such experience is not just play... it is work he must do in order to grow up."

~ Maria Montessori

Table of Contents

Ways to Incorporate this Lesson Plan

Peace education was critical for Maria Montessori her because she lived during the time when the first nuclear bomb was dropped. When Dr. Montessori was alive, all the inhabitants of the earth had this collective experience of facing their mortality at the same time. They realized that we now have a technology that we can use to destroy ourselves within minutes.

She understood that deeply. Her pedagogical approach was not to focus on the problem itself, but to focus on the things that lead up to that problem. We need to go back to the beginning, and the beginning is children.

From the very beginning, you can teach children to collaborate and accept each other. You can show them that human beings are fundamentally the same, and that externalities like the resources we have don't define who we are. Then we have a shot of making it as a species.

Perhaps you have heard the term "cosmic education" to describe the approach Dr. Montessori took in structuring the way she educated her students. This structure is inspired by the notion that life and the things we hold dear is best taught in a circular, rather than a linear fashion. Each year is felt as a chain tethered together that organically moves the child more deeply into the study of the world as a whole and in its parts at his or her own level and pace. Building on the solid foundation established in the primary classroom, the elementary child is eager to explore the whys, hows and what ifs as he or she goes into more detail and expands into related areas of interest.

As you look through the guide, you will notice that each day provides more than you will be able to complete. This allows for some flexibility on your part. You can give lessons to those students who are in their second or third year or you can incorporate the lessons at a more appropriate time based on the age and maturity level of your community. This allows you to still hold to the tenets of following the children and their interests and needs without losing the ability to prepare the children for the works they will experience in the Elementary classroom. The beauty of the Montessori curriculum is that the lessons are based on the need children have more repetition. So, if you have a child who is in her second or third year, you will soon notice that the spooning work will hold her interest for different reasons than what piqued her interest in her first year in the Primary classroom. Look at this curriculum at the skeleton by which to spark your own interest in how to approach your classroom.

The few first weeks of the curriculum are geared to the three-year olds entering the classroom. Children who are returning to the classroom will be delighted by the many works they have been introduced to and will have the ability to begin their work time. You may have some who are ready to be the leaders and mentors in your classroom which will help them to grow in their abilities while at the same time build community to the new children in the classroom who may feel a bit nervous to be in this new setting. Older children who are new to the Montessori environment may have passed the sensitive period for many of the earlier sensorial and practical life materials but returning children who have mastered those materials often find it comforting to use then again while waiting for their new lessons.

The curriculum integrates practical life, grace and courtesy. Peace curriculum, sensorial, math language, science, botany, zoology, geography, music, yoga body awareness, and art into a meaningful yearly theme. As Dr. Montessori emphasized, it is essential to be spontaneous and sensitive to the needs and interests of the child. Select, adapt, rearrange, expand, minimize, omit and merge these ideas with your own. A single page may be expanded upon for an entire week or omitted entirely. Journaling, observing and following the child, and modifying these monthly curriculums are important components for their use.

As you look through the pages of the curriculum, you will notice a letter in parenthesis next to each lesson (bolded for emphasis) after each work to assist in easily recognizing what part of the curriculum you are engaging: (P-practical life, S-sensorial, M-Math, T-Time Line, History and Great Lessons, L-language, G-pre-geography and geography, SCI-science, B-botany, A-Art).

Most schools begin the school year with most of the Montessori materials removed from the work shelves, introducing each lesson one at a time. Basic generic materials are on the shelf which the children are free to use at first without a lesson. The lessons listed in bold on each daily page are a suggested sequence for introducing the materials to the work shelves, and not necessarily to be presented to all children at the same time, but to those children who are ready. Each lesson is given according to the child's readiness so the pace and sequence may vary slightly with the individual child. Lessons are given individually or as a small group according to the needs and abilities of the children, the particular work or personal or school philosophy.

Each day, the children are allowed an uninterrupted work period where they can work undisturbed and receive one on one lessons. Begin the year with a short work time and increase it gradually to 3 hours. The work period is filled with movement. A piece of work may involve returning to the shelf several times. This is the movement Dr. Montessori intentionally built into the lessons. The children are allowed freedom to walk around while finding the next material to work with and have the option of a quiet place such as a reading corner for a quiet break. The extended/outside classroom is accessible from the inside classroom and offer activities such as woodworking and gardening.

The times given for circle, group and work periods are a sample schedule to be adapted to your school's routine and the children's needs. Present a circle (or not) according to the natural flow of the classroom, respecting the uninterrupted work period and modifying them according to the changing interests and the needs of the children. Be in the moment. Integrate other ideas and subjects of interest to you and the children. Having a genuine joy and enthusiasm for the topic of study while being natural and spontaneous is an integral element of Montessori.

Montessori taught that the first job of the teacher is to prepare an environment where the child can teach herself and develop self-discipline. The classroom and its materials, plants, and animals are enthusiastically cared for by the children. Perhaps the most difficult tenet the Montessori classroom director is asked to embody is to become invisible enough to allow this to occur.

A Discussion about your Language Album

In the September, October and November Guides, all letters were introduced. Over the next month, you will begin to gather data based on the introduction of all letters to your students. Some students will not show much interest. Many of your 3-year olds may spend most of their time in Practical Life and Sensorial or in your Outdoor Environment. Because you will continue to build vocabulary and awareness of sound through singing, conversations and lessons given, the students will continue to build interest for your language area.

In the meantime, focus can shift to those students that have increased interest in learning their letters, building letter sound awareness and building stamina to sound out words and start to read. In my environment, I have a sound table where I can work with the child one on one and gauge where each one is at and track the growth in this area. Each one has a Sound Book that has a page with each one of the lowercase letters listed on the page – place them in the book in random order rather than "a, b, c" order. I will sit with a child and go through the book until we have three sounds that the child is unaware of. I take those 3 letters and do a three-period lesson with the sandpaper letters. I also have a box of sand that I use to have them trace the letters in the sand. Finally, I have a small booklet labeled "secret message" that I send home with the three-letter sound that I want the child to work on at home. I proceed in this way until the child has about 90% grasp of the letter sounds. Then I begin to transition the child into the AMS Language system of Pink, Blue and Green reading system and couple that with BOB books.

Montessori Basics: Pink, Blue, and Green Series

The Pink, Blue, and Green Series work is an integral part of Montessori language. Many people have questions about these materials, though. They don't seem quite as self-explanatory as other common Montessori work. There's a lot to know about the history and usage of these materials – so read on for more info!

When Maria Montessori began working with the children in the first Casa dei Bambini (Children's House), she gave them sandpaper letters to trace while saying the correct sound. She didn't do any specific work in the area of reading, but almost effortlessly, the children began to read. Italian is a very phonetic language (words are spelled the way they sound), and once the children knew the sounds, they could read.

After the Montessori method was brought to the United States in the 1920s, it was clear that another approach was needed to teach reading and writing in English. While there are many phonetically spelled words in English, there are even more that use "phonemes"; that is, groups of letters that create distinct sounds when combined. For instance, "ough" can make several sounds, as in "through" or "bough". These sounds need to be memorized; they can't be sounded out phonetically.

The Pink, Blue, and Green Series materials were developed to meet that need. They break down the essentials of English phonics into three groups: short vowel sounds, consonant blends, and phonetic combinations. By moving through these materials in order, a child can easily master the art of reading and writing in English.

The Pink Series materials are where it all begins. Pink Series words consist of three letters: a beginning and ending consonant, and a vowel in the middle. All the vowel sounds in this series are short vowels: "a" as in "c**a**t"; "e" as in "b**e**d", "i" as in "p**i**g", "o" as in "h**o**t", and "u" as in "b**u**s". The letter "y" is not included in this grouping.

After mastering the Pink Series, the child is ready to move to Blue Series words. These words consist of consonant blends (at the beginning or end of the word, or both), and a short vowel sound. Examples would include "flag", "mend", and "clock". There are about 20 different blends, if you include doubles like "ll" and "ss". The child may work on this step for quite a while, as there are hundreds of words that fit into this scheme (see picture for an example of Blue Series matching cards).

Once the Blue Series words have been mastered (essentially, that means the child is familiar with all the blends and can spell most Blue Series Words), they are ready for Green Series. The Green Series is where reading fluency really begins, as the child now has the keys to unlock the inconsistencies and idiosyncrasies of the English language.

The Green Series words consist of all the major phonemes, for example: "ai", "ou", "ie", and "ow". It also includes vowel combinations with a consonant in the middle, like "a_e" or "i_e" where the "_" is a consonant. These would be words like "c**ake**" or "m**ice** ". It includes silent letters, hard and soft letters, and many other difficult spellings and reading challenges. There are about 40-50 different sound combinations in this group.

There is a huge variety of Pink, Blue, and Green Series work. Common ones include matching cards, rhyming cards, using the movable alphabet to spell words, cards with lists of words for spelling or reading practice, and word cards with matching objects. Materials differ by classroom and teacher and most Montessori companies have their own personalized sets of materials that are all slightly different.

Pink, Blue, and Green Series materials are easy to make at home; for suggestions, check out this post:

What Can You Do with the Language Basics?

The great thing is, most Montessori materials have multiple uses for different age groups. So, here are a few things you can do with the Language Basics:

Beginning set up for 6-9 language:

Pink, blue, & green series materials
Word study materials
Movable alphabet

The Pink, Blue, & Green series materials should include word lists or spelling cards, and pictures and objects of Pink, Blue, & Green series words. Pictures can be photos, clipart, or even cut out of books or magazines. Objects can be easily found around the house or classroom; here's some suggestions:

Pink Objects
pen
nut
jet (toy airplane)
bag (small gift bag)
cup
bus
map (print a small one off the internet & laminate)
peg (from lite brite)
rug (a small oval of fabric)
top (toy that spins)
box (small jewelry box)
animals from a farm or play set: cat, dog, fox

Blue Objects:
ball
bell

block (wooden toy)
brush (paint or hair)
clip (paper clip)
rock
flag
ring
shell
sock & shoe from a doll

Green Objects:
spool
leaf
rose
dime
cube (square block)
bead
soap (hotel-sized bar)
seed
globe

Okay, now that you've assembled some Pink, Blue, & Green materials, you need a movable alphabet. Those can be easily stored in a plastic tackle box (find that at a craft or hobby store).

The child can use the objects and/or pictures to spell words, rhyme words, and write stories – all with the movable alphabet. Have them take all the objects from one set, put them on their rug, and spell each one out with the movable alphabet. Or, choose one object, spell it, and then think of 2-3 words that rhyme with it and spell those out too. Or, have the child spell the color of each object.

The word lists or spelling cards can be used as story starters, spelling tests (both written and oral), spelling bees, and alphabetization practice. Pink, Blue, and

Green series words can also be looked up in the dictionary for dictionary practice.

Word Study materials should include title cards that say "masculine/feminine", "short vowel/long vowel", "person/place/thing", and "singular/plural". The child can use the movable alphabet or slips of scrap paper to write appropriate words for each category. Other word study cards include compound word matching, homophones, prefix/suffix, and contractions.

These materials – and the variations contained within – could easily be used for the first few months of school for 6-9-year olds. Stories written with the movable alphabet could be written on paper in cursive by older students; either they could turn it into cursive on their own, or use a cursive movable alphabet to start with (naturally the difficulty of the story itself will increase as the child's age increases)

Handwriting

I highly recommend coupling a program called "Handwriting Without Tears" with your curriculum. My director paid for the Lead Teachers to go through the course. They are usually offered ½ day or full day. You are given all the materials to use in the classroom setting. What I loved about the course is that it broke uppercase and lowercase letters into 4 components: long lines, short lines, big curves, little curves. The handwriting of the students changed DRAMATICALLY using these simple cues and the wood shapes that come with the workshop. I would offer group lessons with chalkboards and I can easily say that this one of the high points of the child's day.

CLICK HERE for more information

Calendar Time/Star Student of the Week

The prior guides introduced the main components of a traditional calendar time:

- Days of the week
- Months of the year
- Weather

You may want to consider adding this your group time. This is a kindergarten requirement in many States.

You may also want to consider a *"Student of the Week"* option where a child works at home on a list of questions and the family gathers pictures and creates a poster presentation of the information. Each day the child has an opportunity to answer 1-2 questions a day at your groups time and talk about the picture that represents that part of his/her history. This incorporates many of the story telling lessons you find in your Language Album. It also allows for new friends to be made based on common interests and shared backgrounds/ideas/traditions.

CLICK HERE for the kit that I have created.

Geography Home Based Projects

I LOVE finding ways to extend what we learn in the classroom to home conversations and field trips and travel. I find that Geography is a fantastic way to spark this interest. Many children have the opportunity to travel. Some children have been born or have lived in other countries, even on other continents. This is the opportunity to bring world connectedness to the classroom.

The beginning of the month I will send home a newsletter with some suggestions based on the continent we will study. This is simply a starting point and many of the ideas will be sparked when I use the kits that I have made for each continent. The child can bring in artifacts from their family's belongings or put together an age appropriate presentation (no more than 5 minutes) to present in class. If a parent would like to handle the presentation, I suggest that you offer some parameters because you will find many parents will create a presentation appropriate for ADULTS not preschool children.

When the child brings something to share, depending on the age of the child, I will ask her/him to also gather three facts to share with the group.

North America kit

South America Kit

Europe Kit

Asia Kit

Topics We Introduce in March:

Asia

Amphibians

Reptiles

Spring

Johnny Appleseed

St. Patrick's Day

Reading

Planting

Nature Exploration

SPECIAL DATES DURING MARCH*

March 2 --Read Across America Day
March 11--Johnny Appleseed Day
March 12--Plant a Flower Day
March 17--St. Patrick's Day
March 20--First Day of Spring
March 30--Take a Walk in the Park Day

*Make sure to coordinate with the year's calendar to confirm EXACT dates

March Book List

Spring

When Spring Comes, by Kevin Henkes
Bunny's First Spring, by Sally Lloyd-Jones
The Twelve Days of Springtime: A School Counting Book, by Deborah Lee Rose
The Thing about Spring, by Daniel Kirk
Spring Song, by Barbara Sueling
Spring Is Here, by Will Hillenbrand
Spring Is Here, by Taro Gomi
Splish, Splash, Spring, by Jan Carr
My Spring Robin, by Anne Rockwell
Mouse's First Spring, by Lauren Thompson
It's Spring! By Linda Glaser
It's Spring! by Samantha Berger and Pamela Chanko

Continents

Montessori: Map Work by Bobby George and June George
Counting the Continents by Ellen Mitten
National Geographic Kids Beginner's World Atlas by National Geographic
The ABCs of Continents by Bobbie Kalman

Reptiles

Reptiles and Amphibians by Roger Priddy

Usborne Pocket Books: Reptiles

Snakes (Usborne Beginners) by James MacLaine

Sea Turtles by Gail Gibbons

Komodo Dragons by Ruth Bjorklund

The Mixed-Up Chameleon by Eric Carle

A Color of His Own by Leo Lionni

Verdi by Janell Cannon

I Wanna Iguana by Karen Kaufman Orloff

Amphibians

Alligators All Around by Maurice Sendak
Brief Thief by Michael Escoffier, illustrated by Kris Di
Giacomo
Chameleon Sees Colors by Anita Bijsterbosch
Crictor by Tomi Ungerer
The House on East 88th Street by Bernard Waber
If You Ever Want to Bring an Alligator to School, Don't! by
Elise Parsley
Herman and Rosie by Gus Gordon
Lizard from the Park by Mark Pett
One Cool Friend by Toni Buzzeo, illustrated by David
Small
The Watermelon Seed by Greg Pizzoli

GETTING TO KNOW YOU/STUDENT OF THE WEEK

The Pigeon Has to Go to School by Mo Willems
School's First Day of School by Adam Rex and Christian
Robinson
Brown Bear Starts School by Sue Tarsky and Marina Aizen
Pirates Don't Go to Kindergarten! by Lisa Robinson and
Eda Kaban
The King of Kindergarten by Derrick Barnes and Vanessa
Brantley-Newton
The Day You Begin by Jacqueline Woodson
All Are Welcome by Alexandra Penfold
We Don't Eat Our Classmates by Ryan T. Higgins

You're Finally Here! by Melanie Watt
First Day Jitters by Julie Danneberg
The Name Jar by Yangsook Choi
The Exceptionally, Extraordinarily Ordinary First Day of School by Albert Lorenz The Book with No Pictures by B.J. Novak
How to Get Your Teacher Ready by Jean Reagan

READING

Love You, Hug You, Read to You! by Tish Rabe, illustrated by Frank Endersby
Bunny's Book Club by Annie Silvestro, illustrated by Tatjana Mai-Wyss
Miss Brooks Loves Books! (And I Don't) by Barbara Bottner, illustrated by Michael Emberley
The Mermaid's Purse by Patricia Polacco
Froggy Goes to the Library by Jonathan London, illustrated by Frank Remkiewicz
The Not So Quiet Library by Zachariah Ohora
Wild About Books by Judy Sierra, illustrated by Marc Brown
Look! by Jeff Mack

JOHNNY APPLESEED

Johnny Appleseed by Reeve Landbergh
Johnny Appleseed by Jodie Shepherd
How Do Apples Grow? By Betsey Maestro
The Seasons of Arnold's Apple Tree by Gail Gibbons
Bad Apple: A Tale of Friendship by Edward Hemingway
Apple Farmer Annie by Monica Wellington
Apples. Apples Everywhere by Robin Koontz
Seed by Seed (The legend of Johnny Appleseed) by Esme Raji Codell

ST. PATRICKS DAY

Good Luck Bear by Greg Foley
Jamie O'Rourke and the Big Potato by Tomie DePaola
Leprechauns Never Lie by Lorna Balian
The Leprechaun Trap by David and Kelly Clinch
Lucky Tucker by Leslie McGuirk
The Naughty Leprechaun Story by Stephanie Hicks
Ten Lucky Leprechauns by Kathryn Heling and Deborah Hembrook
St. Patrick's Day by Dorothy Goeller
The Story of the Leprechaun by Katherine Tegen
What is St. Patrick's Day? by Elaine Landau

PLANTING

Lola Plants a Garden by Anna McQuinn
There's a Pest in the Garden by Jan Thomas
The Turnip by Jan Brett
Sunflower House by Eve Bunting
One Bean by Anne Rockwell
Jack's Garden by Henry Cole
Jamie O'Rourke and the Big Potato by Tomie de Paola
How a Seed Grows by Helene Jordan
The Enormous Potato by Aubrey Davis
Tops & Bottoms by Janet Stevens
The Surprise Garden by Zoe Hall
Planting a Rainbow by Lois Ehlert
The Tiny Seed by Eric Carle
Flower Garden by Eve Bunting

NATURE EXPLORATION

Tessalation! by Emily Grosvenor
We're Going on a Bear Hunt by Michael Rosen
Bubble Trouble by Margaret Mahy

The Tiny Seed by Eric Carle
Where the Wild Things Are by Maurice Sendak
Where is the Green Sheep? By Mem Fox
Blueberries for Sal by Robert McCloskey
You Can Be a Nature Detective by Peggy Kochanoff
The Curious Garden by Peter Brown
Everywhere Babies by Susan Meyers

ASIA

Bee-bim Bop by Linda Sue Park, illustrated by Ho Baek Lee
Dim Sum for Everyone! by Grace Lin
Yoko by Rosemary Wells
Dear Juno by Soyung Park, illustrated by Susan Kathleen Hartung
Hot, Hot Roti for Dada-ji by F. Zia, illustrated by Ken Min
The Name Jar by Yangsook Choi
Zen Shorts by John Muth
Wabi Sabi by Mark Reibstein

8:30am Circle: Introduce "Star Student of the Week." Decide how you would like to incorporate it into your calendar time.

This week Red Across America is observed on March. This can be a week full of activities in your classroom or perhaps your school has its own series of events.

Some ideas:

1. Circle Time Stories

Seems simple, but the best way to celebrate this day is to read a good book. Pick out a story or two to be read during circle time for little learners. Older kids and teens can head to the library to pick out a book that interests them. They can read on their own or choose to read to younger children.

2. Visit a Bookstore

Several bookstores hold readings throughout the country to help honor Read Across America Day. Look online for participating bookstores and the dates they hold story time. If there's not a reading near you, talk to your local bookstore and encourage them to partake in the national celebration of reading. In any case, a trip to a bookstore is still a wonderful way to honor this day. This can also be an activity that you encourage your families to do on their own. Even better, visit a library!

3. Costume Party

Commemorate this day with a costume party where everyone can dress up as their favorite character from a beloved book.

4. Pajama Day

Everyone has heard the saying, "curl up with a good book." Give children the chance to do just that by having them come to school dressed in their pajamas and slippers, with their favorite book, and a comfort item, such as a teddy bear or blanket. Set up the reading nook area or the whole classroom to be as comfortable as possible with floor mats, beanbag chairs, pillows, even a tent or two to transform the space. Offer up a few special treats for pajama day including hot chocolate, tea, and a few healthy snack options.

5. Books with a Buddy

The buddy system is an excellent way to learn and share with friends. Help younger children by having older kids, siblings, or relatives come in and pair up to read a good book with them. Encourage switching partners and stories to facilitate more reading time with additional books to celebrate Read Across America Day.

At Circle Time, read a story from the READING selections. Then use this time to discuss with the group what the plans for the week will be.

LESSONS

Famous children's authors 3-part cards

Famous children's books 3-part cards

Parts of a book three-part cards

ART: Create the cover of a book you will write. Include the characters, something about an action in the story and give the book a name.

KidZor

Reading Rocks!

Name: _____

Draw a cover for your favorite book. Don't forget the author and title!

YOGA: choose two poses from the basket

11:30am Circle:

Story Time: Read a book from the **READING** selections.

LESSONS:

STAMP GAME PRESENTATION- MULTIPLICATION*

* Since March has three weeks due to spring break, we will take the time to review old math lessons and stay with multiplication works they we introduced in February.

2:30pm Circle: Read a book from the **AMPHIBIAN** selections

8:30am Circle: Read a book from the **READING** selections. Incorporate Student of the week and whatever activities (classroom or school wide) you have planned for the day.

Lessons:

PARTS OF A FROG 3 PART CARDS

HOW TO READ A BOOK SEQUENCING CARDS

LETTER WRITING WORK

SIGHT WORDS: OR, ONE, HAD, BY, WORD

Create a basket with each of the sight words you have introduced. You can create a matching work, or you can have each student have their own personal set of index cards with the words on them that they can practice together as partner work.

Yoga: choose two poses from the basket

11:30am Circle: Read a book from the **AMPHIBIAN** selections

Experiment: Make an egg float in Saltwater

Materials needed: one egg, water, salt, a tall drinking glass.

INSTRUCTIONS: Pour water into the glass until it is half full. Stir in lots of salt (about 6 tablespoons). Carefully pour in plain water until the glass is nearly full (be careful to not disturb or mix the salty water with the plain water). Gently lower the egg into the water and watch what happens.

What's happening?

Saltwater is more dense than ordinary tap water. The denser the liquid, the easier it is for an object to float in it. When you lower the egg into the liquid, it drops through the normal tap water until it reaches the salty water. At this point the water is dense enough for the egg to float. If you were careful when you added the tap water to the saltwater, they will not have mixed, enabling the egg to amazingly float in the middle of the glass.

2:30pm Circle: Read a Book from the **READING** selections

8:30am Circle: Remember to incorporate Star Student of the week and any Read Across America activities that you have planned. We will introduce our Fourth Continent this month: Asia

YOGA: choose 2 poses from the basket

SONG/MOVEMENT: Five Green and Speckled Frogs

Lyrics:

Five green and speckled frogs

Sat on a speckled log

Eating some most delicious bugs Yum, yum!

One jumped into the pool Where it was nice and cool

Then there were four green speckled frogs Glub, glub

(Count down from 5 to 1)

Video link: CLICK HERE

LESSONS:

PIN POKING ASIA MAP

PRESENTATION ON STAMP GAME: MULTIPLICATION (CONTINUED)

ABCs of ASIA (MY RESOURCE SOLD SEPARATELY- you can incorporate your Geography work as desired here):

A-Angkor Wat

ART: Focus on Artist - Yayoi Kusamen

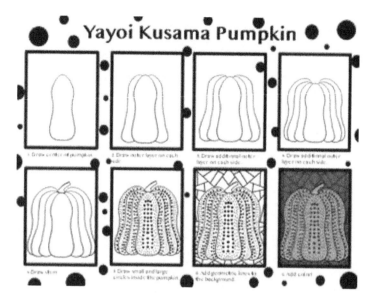

1.

Who is she?

Yayoi Kusama is a Japanese artist who is sometimes called 'the princess of polka dots. Although she makes lots of different types of art – paintings, sculptures, performances and installations – they have one thing in common, DOTS!

What's with all the dots?

Yayoi Kusama tells the story of how when she was a little girl she had a hallucination that freaked her out. She was in a field of flowers when they all started talking to her! The heads of flowers were like dots that went on as far as she could see, and she felt as if she was disappearing or as she calls it 'self-obliterating' – into this field of endless dots. This weird experience influenced most of her later work.

By adding all-over marks and dots to her paintings, drawings, objects and clothes she feels as if she is making them (and herself) melt into, and become part of, the bigger universe. She said:

'Our earth is only one polka dot among a million stars in the cosmos. Polka dots are a way to infinity. When we obliterate nature and our bodies with polka dots, we become part of the unity of our environment'.

Pumpkins

11:30am Circle:

Story Time: Read a book from the **ASIA** selections.

2:30pm Circle: Read a book from **AMPHIBIANS** SELECTIONS.

ABCs of Asia

B- Bokeo Nature Reserve, Laos

Week 1   Thursday   READ ACROSS AMERICA CONTINUES

8:30am Circle: Read one of the books from the **READING** selections.   Continue to implement Star Student of the Week and any Read Across America Activities.   You can also use the sample book cover template and have your students create the book cover of their favorite books.

LESSONS:

ASIA GEOGRAPHY FOLDER

ASIA PLANT/ANIMAL SORTING CARDS

WHAT NUMBER COMES BEFORE____? AFTER? (review)

COMPOUND WORDS (review)

AMPHIBIANS 3 PART CARDS

COOKING: Chicken and Sweet Corn Soup (very similar to egg drop soup you can order at a Chinese food restaurant).
You can add greens to it, my favorite being Chinese broccoli and broccolini, to make it a complete meal. Though this recipe is made with chicken, it is easily made vegetarian/vegan by omitting the chicken.

Ingredients

2 cups (500ml) chicken or vegetable broth/stock
1 can (16oz/420g) creamed corn
1 tsp soy sauce (all purpose or light)
1 tsp ginger, minced or finely chopped
1 garlic clove, minced or finely chopped
1 tsp corn flour / cornstarch, mixed with a splash of cold water
1 egg, whisked
1 cup shredded cooked chicken
Salt and white pepper, to taste

3 tbsp sliced scallions / shallots (optional)

Instructions

1.   Place broth, creamed corn, soy sauce, Chinese cooking wine, ginger, garlic and corn flour water mixture in a saucepan over high heat.

2.   Bring to boil, then turn down the heat to medium and stir occasionally. Cook for 5 minutes or until slightly thickened.

3.   Adjust seasoning with salt, turn off heat, and slowly whisk in the egg so it cooks in "ribbons" throughout the soup. This also thickens the soup.

4.   Add the chicken, season with white pepper, and serve, garnished with scallions.

Makes 4-6 servings

11:30am Circle:

YOGA: choose 2 poses from the basket

Story Time Read a book from the **ASIA** Selections

2:30pm Circle:

Play 1-minute Silence Game or ask the children to close their eyes and listen to some peaceful music for one minute. Talk about peace in association with the land, water and air. What makes them feel peaceful. How do these elements help them to feel peaceful?

Art: Frogs

Week 1   **Friday**   **WHY IS READING IMPORTANT?**

8:30 Circle: Read a story from the **READING** selections. Wrap up this week's STUDENT OF THE WEEK PRESENTATION AND DECIDE WHO IS NEXT WEEK'S STAR STUDENT.

Introduce the 40 book reading challenge

Create a literacy activity or a literacy night where you have a make and take of some type of conduit to log the books the children are reading at home/having read to them. You can have them create a book of 40 pages – does not have to be full pages or even index cards would work – and the child can design the cover and come up with a cool binding. On the log, make sure name of book and author, date read, and what one fact/opinion the child would like to share. Also decide what kind of 'reward' the child should expect for completing the activity.

YOGA: choose two poses from the basket

LESSONS:

Fact or Opinion Language Work

11:30am Circle: Read a story from the **READING** Selections. A FINAL CONVERSATION WITH THIS WEEK'S STAR STUDENT.

EXPERIMENT: Dissolving Sugar at different Heats

Materials: sugar cubes, cold water in a clear glass, hot water in a clear glass, spoon for stirring.

Instructions: Make sure the glasses have an equal amount of water. Put a sugar cube into the cold water and stir with the spoon until the sugar disappears. Repeat this process (remembering to count the amount of sugar cubes you put into the water) until the sugar stops dissolving, you ae at the point where sugar starts to gather on the bottom of the glass rather than dissolving. Write down how many sugar cubes you could dissolve in the cold water. Repeat the same process for the hot water, compare the number of sugar cubes dissolved in each liquid. Which dissolves more?

What's happening? The cold water is not able to dissolve as much water as the hot water. Why? Another name for the liquids inside the cups is a solution. When this solution can no longer dissolve sugar, it becomes a saturated solution, this means that sugar starts forming on the bottom of the cup. The reason the hot water dissolves more is because it has faster moving molecules which are spread further apart than the molecules in cold water. With bigger gaps between the molecules in the hot water, ore sugar molecules can fit in between.

2:30pm Circle: Read a book from the **ASIA** selections.

ABCs of Asia:

C-Chinese Bayberry

D-Dumplings

COOKING: bring various types of dumplings in for a food tasting

Week 1 Art Instructions

Frogs: Materials: cereal box sides, toilet paper rolls, scissors, googly eyes, glue, tempura paints: green and white.

Instructions: Paint two toilet paper rolls with green paint; add some white to create different gradients of green. Let dry. Cut 1 cereal box side into a circle – this will be the background. Paint the circle green and let dry. Cut the toilet paper rolls into circles – you will need 8 circles total. Create the frog using the circles and add the googly eyes.

Yayoi Kusama inspired pumpkins: Materials: watercolor paper, pencils, Q-tips, black paint, sharpie, watercolor paints. (option: do the background or leave it out if time does not permit).
Instructions: See below for the directed line drawing. Use Q-tips and black paint to create the circle patterns in the pumpkins. Another option would be to draw apples instead to prepare for the Johnny Appleseed unit. Also, paint the background and leave the main item (pumpkin or apple) shine with black and white.

Yayoi Kusama Pumpkin

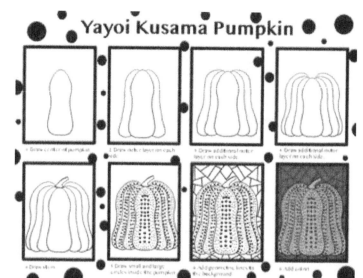

Reflection Journal

A journal is a vital part of the Montessori classroom. This is the space you will use to take notes about what is going well in the classroom and what needs to be tweaked for next week. As you commit to this practice every week, you will find that you have created a very useful diary that will help you learn and grow as a Montessori teacher.

"Establishing lasting peace is the work of education; all politics can do is keep us out of war."
— Maria Montessori

No School

No School

No School

No School

No School

Week 3   **Monday**   **Johnny Appleseed**

8:30am Circle: *INTRODUCE THE STAR STUDENT OF THE WEEK (REVIEW NOTES AT THE BEGINNING OF THE GUIDE AS NEEDED).*

Read a book from the **JOHNNY APPLESEED** selections.

THIS WEEK'S SIGHT WORDS: THERE/USE/AN/EACH/WHICH

-

we have now introduced 50 sight words

History: Johnny Appleseed

ART: Apple mixed media art

COOKING: Applesauce

Ingredients

- 4 apples - peeled, cored and chopped

- ⌐ 3/4 cup water

- ⌐ 1/4 cup white sugar

- ⌐ 1/2 teaspoon ground cinnamon

Directions

1. In a saucepan, combine apples, water, sugar, and cinnamon. Cover, and cook over medium heat for 15 to 20 minutes, or until apples are soft. Allow to cool, then mash with a fork or potato masher.

LESSONS – GIVEN IN THE GROUP OR INDIVIDUALLY:

THE WORLD MAP CARDS   **ASIA THREE PART**

ASIA LIVING/NONLIVING

11:30am Circle: Read a book from the **Asia** selections. Continue to incorporate your materials from your Geography Album pertaining to Asia. You may also purchase my kit on Asia – CLICK HERE.

ABCS OF Asia

E-eggplant

F-fortune cookies

Optional: Have someone bring in fortune cookies to eat with the applesauce.

2:30pm Circle: Read the book from the **JOHNNY APPLESEED** selections

SONG/MOVEMENT:

Lyrics:

Johnny Appleseed
Traditional, Written by: Unknown, Copyright: Unknown

Oh, the Lord's been good to me.

And so I thank the Lord

For giving me the things I need:

The sun, the rain and the apple seed;

Oh, the Lord's been good to me.

Oh, and every seed I sow

Will grow into a tree.

And someday there'll be apples there

For everyone in the world to share.

Oh, the Lord is good to me.

Oh, here I am 'neath the blue, blue sky

Doing as I please.

Singing with my feathered friends

Humming with the bees.

I wake up every day,

As happy as can be,

Because I know that with His care

My apple trees, they will still be there.

The Lord's been good to me.

Week 3   **Tuesday**   **Plant a Flower Day**

8:30am Circle: Continue to implement your handwriting practice becoming more intentional for your 2nd and 3rd year students. Read my section on handwriting at the beginning of this guide. Also, keep in mind the STAR STUDENT OF THE WEEK for your circle time.

Yoga: choose two poses from the basket

GEOGRAPHY: ABCs of Asia

G- Great Wall of China

H-Hornbill

ARCHITECTURE: USE CONVENTIONAL OR UNCONVENTIONAL MATERIALS TO CREATE THE GREAT WALL OF CHINA – THIS CAN BE DONE IN GROUPS.

11:30am Circle: Read a book from the **PLANTING** selections

SCIENCE: Plant seeds and watch them grow.

MATERIALS: fresh seed of your choice: pumpkin seeds, lima beans, pinto beans, apple seeds, a container to hold the soil and your seeds – students can bring in a small pot, water, access to light and heat.

INSTRUCTIONS: fill the container with soil. Plant the seeds inside the soil. Place the containers somewhere warm, sunlight is good but try to avoid too much sunlight, a windowsill is a good spot. Keep the soil moist by watering it every day or as needed. Have the students great a chart to record observations as the seeds germinate and seedlings begin to sprout from the seeds.

2:30pm Circle: Read a book from the **PLANTING** selections.

LESSONS:

Teens Board Review
Hundred Board/Hundred Chain Review
Presentations of Stamp Game – Division

ART: This can be the time you use to create the observation chart for the seed planting.

The next page offers some ideas for inspiring your log

Plant Observation Journal

Ty_____planted_____   Date seeds planted_____

DAY:_____ Notes:	DAY:_____ Notes:
DAY:_____ Notes:	Day:_____ Notes:
DAY:_____ Notes:	DAY:_____ Notes:

Today is: _____

Day # _____

This is what my plant looks like today:

It is _____ tall.

Today I noticed that my plant _____

_____
_____
_____
_____
_____
_____

Plant observations

Date _____

_____
_____
_____

Date _____

_____
_____
_____
_____

control plant

Name _____

Question: How would plant grow if it is given nutrients, water & sunlight?

WEEK ONE

Observations
_____
_____
_____
_____
_____

WEEK TWO

Observations
_____
_____
_____
_____
_____

WEEK THREE

Observations
_____
_____
_____
_____
_____

WEEK FOUR

Observations
_____
_____
_____
_____

8:30am Circle: Read a book from the **PLANTING** selections

SONG & MOVEMENT: Plant a Little Seed

Video: CLICK HERE

ALSO:

Head, shoulders Knees and Toes for Trees

LYRICS:

Roots, trunks, branches, leaves,
Roots, trunks, branches, leaves,
Buds, and fruits, and flowers in the breeze,
Those are the parts of trees!

Head, shoulders, knees, and toes,
No! Trees don't have those!
They have roots, and trunks, And branches and some leaves,
Those are the parts of trees!

Trees, trees, trees,
They're sprouting up from seeds,
Trees, trees are sprouting up from seeds!
See 3 green-tree seeds,
Blowin' in the big-big breeze,
3 green trees sprouting up from seeds!

Roots, trunks, branches, leaves,
Roots, trunks, branches, leaves,
Buds, and fruits, and flowers in the breeze,
Those are the parts of trees!
Eyes, ears, mouth, and nose,
No! Trees don't have those!

They have roots, and trunks, And branches and some leaves,
Those are the parts of trees!

Trees, trees, trees,
They're sprouting up from seeds,
Trees, trees are sprouting up from seeds!
See 3 green-tree seeds,
Blowin' in the big-big breeze,
3 green trees sprouting up from seeds!

Roots, trunks, branches, leaves,
Roots, trunks, branches, leaves,
Buds, and fruits, and flowers in the breeze,
Those are the parts of trees!
Head, shoulders, knees, and toes,
No! Trees don't have those!
They have roots, and trunks,
And branches and some leaves,
Those are the parts of trees!

Video: CLICK HERE

Lessons:

SEASONS OF THE YEAR THREE PART CARDS

TYPES OF REPTILES THREE PART CARDS

YOGA: choose 2 poses from the basket

SCIENCE: What Absorbs More Heat?

MATERIALS: 2 identical drinking glasses or jars, water, thermometer, 2 elastic bands, white piece of paper, black piece of paper

INSTRUCTIONS: wrap the white paper around one of the glasses using an elastic band. Do the same with the black paper and the other glass. Fill the glasses with the exact same amount of water. Leave the glasses out in the sun for a couple of hours before returning to measure the temperature of the water in each.

What's happening? Dark surfaces such as the black paper absorb more light and heat than the lighter ones such as the white paper. After measuring the temperatures of the water, the glass with the black paper around it should be hotter than the other. Lighter surfaces reflect more light, that's why people where people wear lighter colored clothes in the summer; it keeps them cooler.

11:30am Circle: read a book from the **ASIA** selections. Introduce the idea of creating projects at home that represent Asia (see notes at the beginning of the guide on how to create an extension of learning in Geography).

ABCS OF ASIA:

I – INDIA
J - JACKFRUIT

LESSONS:

Addition Dot Board (REVIEW THIS AND SUBTRACTION WORK AS NEEDED)

SIGHT WORDS REVIEW: first 50 words

Fry's First 100 Words

1. the	21. at	41. there	61. some	81. my
2. of	22. be	42. use	62. her	82. than
3. and	23. this	43. an	63. would	83. first
4. a	24. have	44. each	64. make	84. water
5. to	25. from	45. which	65. like	85. been
6. in	26. or	46. she	66. him	86. called
7. is	27. one	47. do	67. into	87. who
8. you	28. had	48. how	68. time	88. am
9. that	29. by	49. their	69. has	89. its
10. it	30. words	50. if	70. look	90. now
11. he	31. but	51. will	71. two	91. find
12. was	32. not	52. up	72. more	92. long
13. for	33. what	53. other	73. write	93. down
14. on	34. all	54. about	74. go	94. day
15. are	35. were	55. out	75. see	95. did
16. as	36. we	56. many	76. number	96. get
17. with	37. when	57. then	77. no	97. come
18. his	38. your	58. them	78. way	98. made
19. they	39. can	59. these	79. could	99. may
20. I	40. said	60. so	80. people	100. part

ART: REPTILE CRAFT

Materials: green, light brown and dark brown felt, buttons, scissors, glue (optional – this can easily be turned into a sewing project in the places where you would glue pieces together).

SONG AND MOVEMENT: I Have a Little Turtle

I had a little turtle.

Cup your hand slightly to make a shell.

He lived inside a box.
Cover the shell with your other hand.

He swam in the water.
Move both arms as if swimming.
And he climbed on the rocks.
Move both arms as if climbing.

He snapped at a mosquito.
Make a snapping motion with one hand.
He snapped at a flea.
Snap again.
He snapped at a minnow.
Snap again.
And he snapped at me.
Snap again.

He caught the mosquito.
Snatch the imaginary bug and eat it.
He caught the flea.
Same as above.
He caught the minnow.
Again.

But he didn't catch me.
Shake your head and wag your finger.

Week 3   **Thursday**   **REPTILES**

8:30am Circle: Read a story from the **REPTILES** selections

LESSONS:

Parts of a turtle 3-part cards

Types of Reptiles 3-part cards

GEOGRAPHY: ABCs of ASIA

K-KUNG PAO CHICKEN

L-LORIS

Cooking/Food Tasting: KUNG PAO CHICKEN – families can be invited to send in their version of KUNG PAO CHICKEN

LESSONS:

ASIA Pin Poking of the map (Big Work)

11:30am Circle- Read a book from the **ASIA** selections.

2:30pm Circle: Read a Book from the **REPTILES** selections

ART: CONTINUE WORKING ON TURTLE CRAFT

Week 3   **Friday**   **ST. PATRICKS DAY**

8:30am Circle: Read a book from the **ST. PATRICKS DAY** selections

Finish spotlight on Star Student of the week; introduce Star Student for next week

Follow the guidelines you or your school have set for St. Patrick's Day

SONG AND MOVEMENT:

LESSONS:

Noun/Verb Game (review)

Addition Bead Frame

ART: Some Craft Ideas for St. Patrick's Day

paper plate
rainbow
ST. PATRICK'S DAY CRAFT

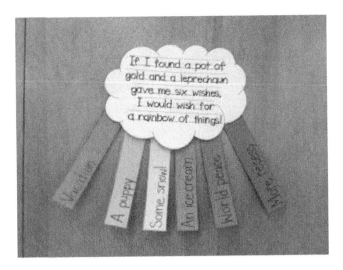

11:30 Circle: Read a story from the **ST. PATRICKS DAY** selections

YOGA: choose two poses from the basket

2:30pm Circle: Read a book from the **ASIA** selections

ABCs of Asia

M-Mekong Delta
N-Napa cabbage

Review all the things we have learned about Asia. Talk about the places the children would like to travel to see and all the places they have gone. Make a brainstorming map for the exercise and date it and add it to your classroom environment.

LESSONS:

Famous Landmarks in your ASIA three-part cards

COOKING: This could be an opportunity to have "green" food to come in from home for St. Patrick's Day.

OR

Easy Green Smoothie Recipe Bowl

This easy green smoothie bowl is creamy from the avocado and packed full of healthy greens and fruits. Top it with almonds, chia seeds and chopped fruit for the perfect start to your day!
Prep Time 5 minutes
Total Time 5 minutes
Servings 2 -3 servings

Ingredients

- 12-15 oz kefir (sub 1/2 milk and 1/2 Greek yogurt if no kefir)

- 2 cups frozen mixed greens or spinach

- 1 avocado

- 4 frozen figs or 1/2 cup other frozen fruit

- 1/2 of a large apple

- 1/2 cup coconut water optional

- 5-6 ice cubes
- Toppings: chopped apple slivered almonds, chia seeds and chopped dates.

Instructions

1. Blend. Top with chopped apple, slivered almonds, chia seeds and chopped dates

Week 3 Art Instructions

<u>Apple mixed media art</u>: Materials: paper plate, red/brown/green construction paper, glue, scissors, brown crayon. Instructions: Tear red construction paper into squares with your hands. Glue the red paper around the edge of the paper plate. Cut out a stem and leaf. Glue onto the back of the paper plate at the edge. Draw seeds in the middle of the paper plate.

<u>Paper plate rainbow with shamrocks:</u> Materials: paper plate, markers, crayons or tempura paint, green construction paper, pencil, yarn, glue, cotton swabs Instructions: Cut a paper plate in half and cut out the center. Paint/color your rainbow. Glue cotton swabs on the ends. Draw out a 4-leaf clover shape and cut them out – 2 sides that will be glued together with yarn in between. Attach yarn to the back of the rainbow.

paper plate
rainbow
ST. PATRICK'S DAY CRAFT

Option 2:

ST. PATRICKS DAY WISHES: MATERIALS: strips of various colors of construction paper, piece of white construction paper, glue, pencil/pen. Instructions: Draw and cut out a cloud. Take 6 strips of construction paper and write phonetically what your wishes are.

Reflection Journal

Maria Montessori combined knowledge, observation and common sense to create an environment that would feed the minds and sprits of the children. This is your charge as a Montessori guide.

8:30 am Circle: Read a book from the **SPRING** Selections.

INTRODUCE YOUR STAR STUDENT OF THE WEEK

SONG AND MOVEMENT:

Spring Song (Tune: The Farmer in the Dell)

The sun is shining bright,
The sun is shining bright,
Oh, how I love the warmth,
The sun is shining bright.

The rain is falling down,
The rain is falling down,
Oh, how I love the sound,
The rain is falling down.

The flowers start to bloom,
The flowers start to bloom,
Oh, how I love the sight,
The flowers start to bloom.

Springtime (to the tune of "are you sleeping?")

I see rain clouds,
I see birds' nest,
Butterflies too!
Flowers Too!

Everything is growing,
the wind is gently blowing,
Spring is here,
Spring is here!

LESSONS:

SIGHT WORDS THIS WEEK: WILL/UP/OTHER/ABOUT/OUT

SIGNS OF SPRING THREE PART CARDS

GARDENING THREE PART CARDS

TYPES OF FLOWERS NOMENCLATURE CARDS

PARTS OF A FLOWER NOMENCLATURE CARDS

Adverb/Verb Game (Review)

ART: Spring collage

11:30am Circle: Read a book from **ASIA** selections –
allow for any presentations made at home.

ABCs of Asia

O-OPO SQUASH
P-PAD THAI

YOGA: Choose two poses from the basket

2:30pm Circle: Read a book from the **SPRING** selections.

LESSONS:

Subtraction Strip Board/Subtraction Lessons (Review)

Week 4 **Tuesday** **ASIA**

8:30am Circle: Read a book from the **ASIA** selections

ANY PROJECTS THE STUDENTS BROUGHT IN CAN BE PRESENTED DURING THIS WEEK

YOGA: Choose two poses from the basket

GEOGRAPHY: ABCs of ASIA

Q-QING
R-RAINBOW FAMILY VILLAGE

LESSONS:

MULTIPLICATION LESSON (REVIEW)

11:30am Circle: Read a book from the **SPRING** selections.

2.　**COOKING:**

Veggie Bouquet

Ingredients

- 1 large carrot
- 1/3 cucumber
- handful green grapes
- handful blueberries
  - To make your vegetable bouquet you'll need just a few supplies; bamboo skewers, flower shaped mini bento cutters and a glass or vase to present them in. I cut my skewers in half using kitchen scissors to make them easier to work with.
  - For younger children, you may want to cut the sharp point off each skewer too.

Method

Peel the carrot, cut the carrot and cucumber into thick slices. Shape into flowers using mini cutters.

To make each flower, first thread a grape onto a skewer. The grape helps to hold the flower in place and stops it from slipping down the skewer.

Add one or two of the cucumber and/or carrot flowers, then top with a blueberry if wanted.

We made a mixture of flowers; some with cucumber and carrot, some with just carrot, some with blueberries and some without.

2:30pm Circle- Read a book from the **NATURE EXPLORATIONS** selections

8:30am Circle: Read a book from **NATURE EXPLORATION** Selections

SCIENCE EXPERIMENT: BUTTERFLY FEEDER (should be prepared outdoors)

MATERIALS: clear plastic cup, hole punch/thumbtack, string/yarn, ballpoint pen, cotton ball, BRIGHT scrapbook paper, glue, water, sugar,

INSTRUCTIONS:

1. Make holes with a thumbtack or hole punch on each side near the rim on the plastic cup. Tie string through the holes.

2. Make a hole in the bottom of the cup using a thumbtack. Widen the hole to about the size of the hole punch's circle. Use the ballpoint pen if needed to widen the hole

3. Push a small cotton ball into the hole, so half is inside the cup and half is poking out of the bottom.

4. Cut out petal shapes from the scrapbook paper and glue the petals around the cotton ball to make a flower.

5. Put nine tablespoons of water in a separate container. Stir in a tablespoon of sugar. Pour the mixture into the cup. Hang the feeder from a branch.

WHAT'S HAPPENING? Sugary water is like nectar, the sweet liquid that butterflies drink from flowers. The bright petals attract butterflies to the feeder. Then they suck the sugary water as it soaks through the cotton ball.

LESSONS:

PARTS OF A BUTTERFLY THREE PART CARDS

SIGHT WORDS: SOME/HER/WOULD/MAKE/LIKE

11:30am Circle:

SONG/MOVEMENT:

Butterfly, Butterfly

Butterfly, butterfly, flutter around.

Butterfly, Butterfly, touch the ground.

Butterfly, butterfly, fly so free.

Butterfly, butterfly land on me.

Butterfly, butterfly reach the sky.

Butterfly, butterfly say goodbye.

5 Little Butterflies

Five little butterflies by the door.
One flew away, then there were four.

Four little butterflies by the tree.
One flew away, then there were three.

Three little butterflies up in the blue.
One flew away, then there were two.

Two little butterflies out in the sun.
One flew away, then there was one.

One little butterfly now all alone.
She was so lonely, she flew home.

2:30pm Circle: Read a book from the **ASIA** selections

ABCs of ASIA

S-SUN BEAR
T-TIGER'S NEST TEMPLE
Pull out the Asia Puzzle Map and review the countries on the map.

8:30am Circle: Read a book from the **YOUR COUNTRY TIMELINE** selections

LESSONS:

ADDITION/SUBTRACTION STORY PROBLEMS (REVIEW)

What do you find in a park? three-part cards

Parks in the U.S. three-part cards (or area that is relevant to you)

Picnic three-part cards

EXPERIMENT: Making Butter

In honor of Take a Walk in the Park Day, which is March 30, we are going to make butter to spread on the bread you might take if you were going on a picnic (the butter will be eaten tomorrow)

Materials:

Clear mason jar with lid, heavy whipping cream, salt, paper towel, dish to hold the butter.

Note: the students can work in teams of 2-4 for this experiment. You will need more jars to accommodate this option.

Instructions:

1. Half fill a clean jar with heavy whipping cream. Add a pinch of salt for taste. Screw the lid on and shake the jar.
2. Shake the jar for about 10-15 minutes, eventually it will separate into a lump

of fat and a milky liquid. (This step the students will need to help each other).

3. Take out the lump and put it on paper towel. Wrap the towel around it and squeeze out any excess liquid.
4. Put the lump on a dish, keep it in the refrigerator. Tomorrow we will spread it on some bread.

11:30AM Circle: Read a book from the **ASIA** selections.

ABCs OF ASIA

U- UNIVERSITY
V-VIETNAMESE DUCK SOUP
W-WAR MEMORIAL OF KOREA

2:30pm Circle: Read a book from the **SPRING** selections.

Week 4   **Friday**   **TAKE A WALK IN THE PARK DAY**

8:30am Circle Read a book from the **NATURE EXPLORATION** selections. Remember to announce the new star Student of the Week.

YOGA: pick one or two poses from the basket

COOKING/FOOD TASTING: BREAD FOR THE BUTTER MADE YESTERDAY

WATERMELON JUICE

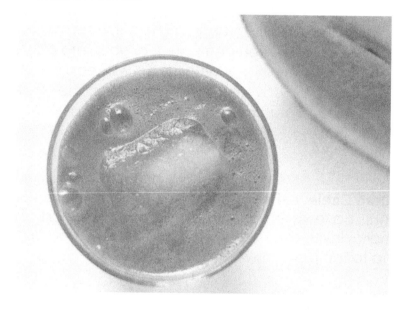

Refreshing, naturally sweet watermelon juice couldn't be easier to make in a blender. Yield will vary based on the size of your watermelon, but my 6.5-pound watermelon yielded about 5 cups of juice.

Ingredients

- 1 small sweet watermelon (a 6 pounder will do)

- 1 small lime, juiced (optional)

Instructions

1. Slice the watermelon in half. Using a big spoon, scoop chunks of sweet watermelon into the blender. Discard the rind.

2. Blend the watermelon until it is totally pulverized. This shouldn't take more than a minute. For extra flavor, squeeze the juice of one small lime into the blender and blend for a few seconds.

3. If your watermelon is notably pulpy or seeded, pour the mixture through a fine mesh strainer into a pitcher. If not, you can pour it directly into glasses filled with ice. Watermelon juice will keep in the refrigerator, covered, for up to 4 days. The juice will separate over time; stir it with a spoon to recombine.

11:30pm Circle: Let's talk about the different parks your students have visited and what they liked the most about the park. Invite the students to plan with their families an outing to the park this weekend.

SONG/MOVEMENT: SHAKE MY SILLIES OUT

We're gonna shake, shake, shake our sillies out, Shake, shake, shake our sillies out, Shake, shake, shake our sillies out, and wiggle our waggles away. We're gonna clap, clap, clap, our crazies out, Clap, clap, clap our crazies out, Clap, clap, clap our crazies out, and wiggle our waggles away. We're Gonna jump, jump, jump our jiggles out, Jump, jump, jump our jiggles out, Jump, jump, jump our jiggles out, and wiggle our waggles away. We're gonna jog, jog, jog our jitters out, Jog, jog, jog our jitters out, Jog, jog, jog our jitters out, and wiggle our waggles away. We're gonna stretch, stretch, stretch our stretchies out, Stretch, stretch, stretch our stretchies out, Stretch, stretch, stretch our stretchies out, and wiggle our waggles away. We're gonna yawn, yawn, yawn our yawnies out, Yawn, yawn, yawn our yawnies out, Yawn, yawn, yawn our yawnies out, and wiggle our waggles away. Repeat all and wiggle our waggles away.

VIDEO: https://www.youtube.com/watch?v=NwT5oX_mqS0

2:30pm Circle: Read a book from the **ASIA** selections

ABCs of ASIA

X-Xi'an

Y-Yak

Z-dZong

GEOGRAPHY: Create one of the structures you have studied so far from the ABCs of Asia using Legos or some other building material.

Week 4 Art Instructions

SPRING COLLAGE: Materials: cupcake liners, pipe cleaners, construction paper, scissors, glue, markers, crayons, watercolor paper 9x12. Instructions: Find some magazine pages of different magazines or perhaps flowers from the school's garden to display and inspire the students as they create their paper collage gardens.

Reflection Journal

What activities did the children really connect with this week? What do you notice about the environment of your classroom? What area of the room did the children experience the most self-motivation? How can you bring that into other areas of the room?

General Instructions

Missing or Broken Pieces

It is important that if any work is missing a piece it is removed from the work shelf until the missing piece are found or replaced. Keep labeled containers of extra pieces in a supply cabinet. The child receives a demonstration, in Montessori language we call this a lesson, before doing a work. Lessons are given without unnecessary talking. Do each step slowly- even more slowly that you can imagine- and deliberately exaggerated movements. This draws the child's attention to your what your hands are doing.

Water work

Make fill lines on the inside of the bowls and pitchers with a permanent marker for control of error for filling various water works. Put on a waterproof apron at the beginning of a water lesson.

Art Lessons

Put on an apron or smock at the beginning of an art lesson if it uses glue or paint. Keep newspaper available for placing under work. Once the easel painting lesson is given, the easel is always available in the classroom.

The Three Period Lesson

The three-period lesson is done when working one on one with a child and is used to introduce new terms or names of things.

Examples of phrasings-

1. "This is a ..."
2. "Show me the ..."

3. Give me the ..."
4. What is this?

Generic Work

Pattern Blocks-wooden or plastic pieces in various geometric shapes.

Puzzle- Look for puzzles with a knob. The knob helps to develop the muscles for holding a pencil. This lesson is given using no words.

Ideas for Lesson Extensions in Each Area of the Classroom

Practical Life Work (and some extensions)

Tongs Sponge Tower – 10 foam sponges of various colors cut in half, tongs. Lesson – using tongs, carefully stack the sponges one on top of the other. When all 10 ae carefully placed.

Paring Socks- this is a basket of children's socks. You can pair them and turn the cuffs.

Parts of the Paintbrush- you can make three-part cards, or you can trace a paintbrush, print the words that are the parts of the paintbrush: handle, ferrule, hairs, tip. Laminate. Have a real paintbrush available as part of the work.

Right and Left shoes- create different shoes – left and right – and laminate it and make is available on the shelf as a pairing/matching work.

Another option: have all the children take off their shoes and put them in the center of the circle. Go around the circle and let a child pick a shoe that is not her own. Find the pair and then place the pair of shoes in front of the child she thinks they belong to.

Sensorial

Color Swatch Matching: Pairs of color swatches from a paint store

Lesson: Put swatches in a pile. Take the top swatch card and put it on the left side of the workspace. Take another card and put it next to the card – is it the same or different color? If yes, place it next to its partner. If no, put it on the right side of the workspace. Continue until all the swatches are matched.

Calendar and Math Work

Calendar Tiles: Age 3+

Purchase 31 one-inch white ceramic tiles. With a permanent marker print the number 1-31. ON paper, make a blank calendar with one-inch squares and laminate.

Lesson-Place the blank calendar on the left. Place the numbered calendar next to it. Have your tiles available. Look at the calendar and place the numbers in the appropriate on the blank calendar using the numbered calendar as your guide.

Calendar Tracing Age 3+

On One copy of the blank calendar as described above, fill in the numerals for the current month and laminate it.

Lesson- Place paper on the calendar and trace the numerals.

Leaf Stair-Press leaves in a leaf press (if available) and then laminate. Number cards 1-5 or 1-10, felt square

Lesson-Place the number cards vertically down the left side pf the felt. Point to and say "1" and place a leaf to the right of the numeral 1. Point to 2 and say "2" and place two leaves to the right. Continue until all the leaves are placed. The control of error is having the exact amount of leaves for the child to place.

Language Work

Preparation for Writing

Practical Life and Sensorial exercises that develop muscles of the fingers and eye/hand and fine motor control- work that involves picking up kernels of popcorn, grasping knobbed puzzles and the knobbed cylinders. It continues with tracing work, insets and sandpaper letters.

Preparation for Reading

Reading begins with silence, listening, sequencing, patterning, naming objects and shapes, matching and classification of objects. It continues with the sandpaper letters and moveable alphabet.

The Silence Game

The Importance of the Silence Game

"One day I had the idea of using silence to test the children's keenness of hearing, so I thought of calling them by name, in a low whisper.... This exercise in patient waiting demanded a patience that I thought impossible."
—Maria Montessori, *The Secret of Childhood*

To Montessori's surprise, when she experimented with this very first Silence Game, the group of over 40 children waited quietly and patiently to hear their names whispered. After they refused the sweets, she thought they might need as a reward, Montessori reflected, "They seemed to say, 'Don't spoil our lovely experience, we are still filled with delight of the spirit, don't distract us.'" Thus, the Silence Game came into being.

Playing the Silence Game can give children a sense of joy, achievement, and social spirit as the group works together for a common goal. It also helps children develop a higher level of self-control, which in turn contributes to the normalization of the classroom. In 1930 Montessori wrote that the Silence Game brings "little by little a discipline composed of calmness and inner beatitude." ("The Importance and the Nature of the Silence Game," *AMI Communications*, 1976)

Indirect Preparation

All the exercises in Practical Life, especially the Grace and Courtesy lessons, are indirect preparation for the Silence Game. Children learn to control and perfect their movements: pushing in a chair quietly and carefully, walking around a work rug on the floor, pouring the rice carefully without the sound of even one grain spilling on the table.

These activities help children develop concentration and precision, as well as social awareness, as they wait for their turn, without disturbing the classmate who is working. They learn to speak softly in response to the teacher's quiet voice, and to stop moving and listen when a chime is rung, or the lights are turned off.

Direct Preparation

Here are some games that can be played to help children perfect the ability to listen and to still the body:

> Pass a bell around the circle, encouraging the children to not let it ring.

Invite children to listen to the sound of birds singing or the rain striking the windowpanes.

Have the children close their eyes. Then play several familiar instruments (egg shaker, rhythm sticks, cymbals). Ask them to identify, by the sound, which instrument was played.

Invite a small group of children to sit quietly with their eyes closed for a short amount of time (start with 20-30 seconds). Afterwards discuss what sounds they heard.

When Are Children Ready?

The Silence Game is best suited for children ages four and up. It should not be attempted until there is certainty of success, and for many classrooms that may be sometime in the spring after months of preparation. You'll know that the children in your classroom are ready to play the Silence Game when they can:

- Control their movements.

- Sit quietly and listen for a period of time.

- Concentrate and work independently.

- Cooperate with each other.

Don't be discouraged if one or two children aren't able to be quiet enough to participate. Your classroom assistant could work with them on a special project outside the classroom.

Playing the Silence Game

Many teachers first introduce the Silence Game when the whole class is gathered, in order to explain and practice the game. Older children can model how to get up, ever so quietly, and go to the teacher once their name is called.

Some teachers choose to hold up a card during the work period that reads "Silence" and then wait, as one-by-one, the children notice, stop working, and become still and silent. Some teachers encourage the children to close their eyes. Then the teacher goes to a far corner or walks out of the room to whisper the children's names. When a child hears her name, she goes over to the teacher and sits near her.

When all the children have heard their whispered names and come to you, you might want to take them outside for a celebratory walk in the garden. Be creative and vary the activities you do after playing this game: group singing, a birthday celebration, or simply a return to work.

Today we live in a noisy world, filled with the sounds of the television, electronics, phone conversations, leaf blowers, sirens, and traffic. Many of us rarely have the opportunity to experience silence or to savor the quieter sounds of bees buzzing, wind rustling the leaves, or a fire crackling in the fireplace. The Silence Game can give children a precious gift that could last a lifetime: the ability to cultivate and appreciate silence.

Felt Patterning

A pattern is a series of repeated lines or shapes

Preparation: Felt strips with felt shapes arranged in a pattern sequence and glued on.

Supplies: Felt shapes of various colors, and long horizontal felt strips

Lessons- place felt shapes in a jar or small basket. Long horizontal strips are used as the space to place the varying patterns and the child has the opportunity to create her own patterns.

Felt Circles- various sizes and colors

Lesson- we are working on gradation of size so if for example you have a red circle, you need to have red circles of differing sizes. This will introduce language as "small, smaller, smallest" or "larger, largest, etc."

Sandpaper Rubbings- use the metal insets to trace the shapes on sandpaper. Cut them out.

Lesson: Place a sandpaper shape on the table rough side up. Place a paper on top. Rub with the side of a fat crayon

Chalk Board – small chalkboard and chalk. Make lines from left to right. Say "left to right." Fill the board with lines. Erase. Make lines top to bottom. Say "top to bottom." Fill the board with lines, Erase.

Matching Cards- pairs of picture to picture cards to be matched. These are also known as three-part cards. It can be played as partner game and as a matching game with the cards turned upside down.

Parts of a … Nomenclature cards (as Parts of a … Book)

Parts of an object such as "parts of an insect" which are simplified drawing in which a child can break down each part of the simple line drawing. The child will color the specific part of the object one at a time, isolating the part and then the name of the specific part is written on the page. Make sure to make enough copies to accommodate the number of parts.

Matching Letters-make pairs of cards with the lower-case letters s-m-a-t. As each set of letters is introduced, they may be used in combination with previously introduced letter. Sets of letters are: smat, fbox, hnde, cpur, wigl, zkqyv. Mix the letters and match in pairs. It can also be played as a memory game. This will be a great way to utilize sandpaper letters if you have them available.

Name tracing- Make a name card- write or print the child's first and last name on a piece of paper and laminate it. Cut pieces of tracing paper the same size as the card. Two clothespins or paper clips, pencil.

Lesson: Place the paper on the name and clip in place. Trace the name. Use with the sandpaper letters if you have them available to practice how the strokes are done.

Season sorting cards –

Preparation of the work: Find or take pictures of children that match the seasons and give representations of seasons changing. Have at least 4 pictures to represent each season. Make four season cards: a simple leaf drawing with the word "Fall" on the back, snowflake with the word "winter," flower with the word "spring," and sun with the word "summer," – laminate all cards.

Lesson- this is a sorting work to be placed in a basket.

Botany

Leaf Press (can be used for flowers as well)

Materials:

- 1 medium sized corrugated cardboard box

- 12 pieces of printer/copy paper

- Rubber bands (at least 2 thick rubber bands) – extra-large file folder rubber bands work great

- Scissors

- Markers or crayons

- Stickers (optional)

1. Help your child cut out six (6 inches by 6 inches) pieces of cardboard box.

2. Next, cut out twelve (6 inches by 6 inch) pieces of paper.

3. Put the press together by alternating the cardboard and papers.

4. Encourage your child to decorate the top layer with their name, stickers or designs. Then go outside to find some interesting leaves, plants and blossoms.

5. Fill the press by putting leaves and flowers between the paper layers of the press. You may want to add notes on the paper about where and when you found the nature items.

6. Secure your press with the rubber bands. Keep the items in the press for about two weeks.
   Other ideas:

7. – Used recycled newspaper instead of printer paper.

8. – Use a glue stick to glue your dried flowers to construction paper to make bookmarks or cards.

9. – Make a dried flower window display. Preserve your dried flowers in between two pieces of clear contact paper. Cut the contact paper into a circle or trim off the edges to make a neat rectangle or square. Hang your creation in a window or put it on your refrigerator for display.

Using the Lesson Plan in a 3-6-year-old classroom

The Children's House is the core of the Montessori Method and is the curriculum of the 3 – 6-year-old child. These classrooms are the starting place, and mainstay, of Montessori education around the world. Developmentally, children at this age need to explore and discover in order to address their insatiable curiosity. These children possess an Absorbent Mind.

Our early childhood classrooms are specifically designed to stimulate and engage children's senses. Each classroom has two adults: a teacher with a unique role accompanied by an assistant. With careful guidance from their teacher, children have the freedom to work independently based on their interests. MSB's distinctive learning environments are aesthetically inviting with an array of learning materials, plants, animals, art, music and direct access to nature. Specially designed, hands-on materials that engage children in learning are everywhere. When children are provided self-direction, and learn through self-discovery, they cultivate strong characteristics such as motivation, concentration, self-discipline and a genuine love of learning.

Children around the age of 3 begin school in the morning program, ending at 11:30. Once a child is ready to stay for lunch, around the age of 4, they may remain at school until 12:30. Once a child turns 5 they may join the extended day program and are dismissed at 2:45.

A Learning Community

The Children's House is a place where children, 3 – 6 years old, can work at their own tempo and follow their curiosities without interruption. It is a place where they can feel at home. Our Early Childhood Program consists of mixed-age classrooms, taking full advantage of the crossover within the developmental stage between 3 and 6 years. Children learn to cooperate with children of different ages and to respect each other's efforts. They learn to care for themselves, aid others and be conscious of their environment. The classroom is a microcosm, a flourishing community where children display, and are shown, respect and dignity.

An Environment Built for Learning

Above all else, our classrooms are prepared with the child in mind. The physical space and routines are harmonized to enhance exploration and independent learning. The room is set up at child height, enabling children to reach what they want without relying on adult help. We believe that children learn more by direct experience and less by simply listening to an adult talk. Our specially designed Montessori materials are simple, elegant and stimulating. They appeal specifically to the child at this stage of development. This prepared environment only includes items that will engage children and encourage spontaneous activity. Each classroom also has an equivalent outdoor footprint to enhance children's' sense of our interconnectedness with nature.

Curriculum

Our daily work in the classroom is clearly defined by a challenging Montessori curriculum that is composed of:

Art, Botany, Drama, Environmental Studies, Geography, Geometry, Language, Mathematics, Music, Practical Life, Sensorial Activities, Practical Life

The exercises of Practical Life provide the foundation for all other activities in the Montessori classroom, fulfilling the child's plea: "Help me to do it myself!" Through exercises in daily living, such as pouring and scrubbing, sewing and gardening, or practicing grace and courtesy, the child gains confidence and mastery of the environment, after individual skills are refined, children apply them in purposeful work, such as serving juice or polishing. Specifically, these activities contribute to the control and coordination of movement, development of concentration, and the self-esteem that comes with making a real contribution to the group.

Pouring & Transferring

Grasping a handle and pouring water or grains helps children develop fine motor control. These simple activities isolate single skills children will later need, in combination, for more complex processes. One principle behind the activities Montessori designed was that "control of error" be evident. Children learn to correct themselves in their work, eliminating the need for adults to point out mistakes. In this spirit, most of the pitchers and dishes we offer are breakable.

Washing & Cleaning

A basic premise behind Maria Montessori's philosophy of early childhood education was that every child is eager for work, even when the work seems like chores to the adult. Through the activities of Practical Life, children not only perform a task; they are also forming foundations on which to organize skills and intelligence. Nowhere is this premise more evident than in Washing and Scrubbing exercises. Through these activities, children develop concentration, become aware of order and sequencing, gain control over their movements, become more independent, and learn to care for their surroundings.

Polishing

A Primary Montessori classroom without polishing activities would be as dull as tarnished silver! Children feel a sense of accomplishment when they see an object fade behind a coating of polish and then reappear all shiny—after a little rubbing, of course. Polishing activities give children a chance to synthesize preliminary skills, such as making a cotton swab and using an eye dropper, into an orderly sequence that yields such a satisfying result. With plenty of polishing variations on the shelf, your children will be shining all year.

Manipulatives

In *The Secret of Childhood*, Montessori wrote that the human hand... *"not only allows the mind to reveal itself but enables the whole being to enter into special relationships with its environment."* Manipulative activities like these engage hands and eyes in a practical task that satisfies the child's need for purposeful work. At the same time, such activities offer unique physical challenges that help children develop concentration and learn to coordinate their most important "tools": eyes and hands!

Food Preparation

When children begin to internalize the foundations of Practical Life, they seek ways to use their skills and assume broader responsibilities. Preliminary activities that isolate single skills demonstrate children's amazing ability to handle kitchen tools. Preparing and serving snacks (and even meals) is a natural way for children to learn cooperation and experience community. Where kitchen facilities are limited, create cooking and clean-up areas with a toaster oven, cutting boards, basins, and pitchers.

Sensorial

Children from birth to age six are in their "sensitive period" for exploring the world through their senses. Maria Montessori encouraged us to provide children with many opportunities to organize the sensory impressions they've been receiving since birth. By your careful selection of items of different textures, colors, sizes, and geometric shapes, children will discover relationships and exclaim, "This bolt is a hexagon," or "This cloth is rough." Sensorial experiences also indirectly prepare children for future exploration of language, mathematics, geometry, art, and music.

Language

Montessori perceived the miracle of language development as "a treasure prepared in the unconscious, which is then handed over to consciousness, and the child, in full possession of his new power, talks and talks without cessation."

Absorbing and perfecting language depends on human contact, but language is not taught. Words are the labels for our experiences. A child who has varied experiences and is given the words for those experiences will develop a well-rounded means of expression. Just as a rich vocabulary is dependent on the child's experience, the transition to reading and writing is dependent on a strong vocabulary. Soon, the child, explorer of the world, will be able to express thoughts and understand and interpret the thoughts of others.

Math

We are providing you with an overview of the Primary Montessori Math Program so that you have a better overall picture of the progression of materials and lessons.

Math is logic, sequence, order, and the extrapolation of truth. In the Montessori philosophy it's stated that the child has a 'mathematical mind' and an internal drive to understand the environment around them. It can therefore be said that children have an inborn attraction for math. Their minds are full of energy that propels them to absorb, manipulate, classify, order, sequence, abstract, and repeat. These tendencies are those which help the child to acquire a greater depth to his mathematical knowledge.

It is the precision of the presentations and the exactness of the math materials that attract children to this area of the classroom. As well, children in the primary Montessori classroom are in the process (sensitive period) of fine tuning their perceptions. Children are sensitive to minute changes in order, sequence, and size. They will notice a teeny tiny bug in the crack of the sidewalk where as adults will walk by blindly without notice.

The exercises in the math area offer the children the 'keys' that they will need to send them on the road to further exploration and maturation of the mathematical mind. The ways in which the materials are ordered allows the children to complete full intellectual cycles that help them to achieve the freedom to become independent.

Math in the primary classroom is made up of many little details that form a whole, but each detail is complete unto itself. All early math exercises are worked at the sensorial level to ensure that the child relates the quantity to the symbol (example: Spindle Boxes).

Botany

Botany studies begin with a look at the life cycle of plants and presentations which explore the importance of plants to human and animal life. Students are encouraged to look at the many ways that plants provide for our fundamental needs. They do this with a variety of independent research projects. Botany studies continue with presentations of nomenclature and impressionistic charts which detail the basic needs of plants, their parts, and the functions of these parts. Students study roots, stems, leaves, flowers and fruits. They learn about plant reproduction, pollination, phyllotaxis, photosynthesis, monocotyledons and dicotyledons, succulent and dehiscent fruits, seeds and the means by which they travel, and alternate means of regenerating. They learn about the system of scientific classification with materials such as the Five Kingdoms Chart and the Plant Classification Chart.

All botany studies are supported by experiments that illustrate how the plant meets its needs, how plant systems function, and the importance of plants to the ecosystem. Students are actively involved in growing, caring for and observing plants in the classroom. Botany work also parallels studies in geography, history and zoology that explore the role of plants on Earth. It is our goal that the children understand, from these studies, the interdependence of all life forms and the custodial role humans must assume to protect and preserve life on Earth.

Geography

One of the many gifts a Montessori education often brings is a life-long enthusiasm for geography. Geography helps children place themselves on Earth, fostering care for the rivers, forests, oceans, and peoples. Physical geography focuses on the features of Earth's environment. Political geography studies how humans have adapted to the land, emphasizing settlement and activity.

Geography is the most all-encompassing subject in the Montessori "cultural curriculum." It creates the foundation for understanding the oneness of the human family, recognizing the basic needs that all people share while appreciating the diversity of how different cultures satisfy those same needs.

Physical and Political Geography

We begin with physical geography, introducing three- and four-year-olds to the Globe of Land and Water (Sandpaper Globe). The sandpaper land is rough to the touch; the oceans are smooth. *"This is how we see Earth from the sky. This is land. This is water."*

We also introduce children to Land and Water Forms, a Practical Life exercise in geography. As the child pours water into the forms, she has the sensorial impression of, for example, an island and a lake. Naming the landforms using three-part cards and learning the definitions of landforms follow.

The materials in the primary classroom for political geography include the Globe of the Continents (Painted Globe) and the Puzzle Map of the World (typically introduced as a sensorial work), along with the Continent Maps, outline maps, and the flags.

Introducing Maps

Once children have worked with the globes, we introduce maps. This transition from globe to map is often difficult for a child. You can compare the Globe of the Continents to the Puzzle Map of the World, identifying each continent on the globe, then the map. You could say, "*A map is an important tool to show what a big place looks like from up high.*" Perhaps you could demonstrate how to make a flat map of the spherical world by letting the air out of an inflatable globe to flatten it. Then compare it to the Puzzle Map of the World.

Five- to nine-year-olds might enjoy drawing maps of their school playground, the lizard's terrarium, or the route from home to school. A treasure map leading to a hidden command card or object in the classroom can encourage map-reading skills.

Exploring the Continents

Most teachers spend hours researching and gathering artifacts to present the physical and political geography of each continent in turn. Storytelling and photographs can bring the countries and continents to life as we introduce children to:

- three-part cards of the people, landmarks, flora, and fauna.

- climates and biomes. Discuss how these affect the clothing people wear and the foods they eat.

- languages, songs, stories, religions, holidays, and foods. Invite parents with knowledge of another country to share their culture.

- artwork, clothing, and instruments.

- physical and political maps.

- the significance of the colors and symbols on flags. Children can make and color flags.

My Bio

Hello! My name is Robin Norgren and I feel honored to be a part of the Montessori community. I come with almost 20 years' experience in management and a love of education and creativity and believe that lifelong learning is key to navigating the world we live in.

I was born in Wurzburg, Germany where my dad was stationed with the U.S. Army. I spent most of my childhood in Detroit, Michigan but moved to Arizona when I was 14 years old.
I have been married for 16 years and my husband has proudly served in the U.S. Navy for almost 20 years, so I have been privileged to have traveled quite a bit. I have two children, a boy and a girl ages 29 and 12. The oldest is in the U.S. Air Force and currently stationed in North Korea and the youngest is excited to start Junior High.

I attended Arizona State University and earned my Bachelor of Science degree in business management and worked in retail for about 15 years and really enjoyed mentoring and training young employees not just about work but life.

When I met my husband, we had dreams of being in the military together which is why I attended Fuller Theological Seminary and earned my degree in Theology with aspirations of becoming a chaplain. But God had other plans and weeks after my candidate packet was rejected, we found out we were pregnant with our youngest. Due to the world's political climate during that time, we decided to rethink how our family would move forward since he was beginning to be deployed for long periods of time. I had a friend who talked highly about Montessori with me throughout the years so I investigated it further and decided this might be a beautiful next step.

I began my AMI certification and unfortunately had to put it on hold when my husband was reassigned to Virginia, so I took my AMS certification and completed it in 2016. I am still in the process of completing my AMI certification because I find both offer a deep and rich understanding of Montessori not simply as an education process but as a lifestyle and a worldview.

I also am passionate about art education and have created programs that I have taught in both Arizona and Virginia to pre-k to 6th grade classrooms. Because I have worked in a Reggio Emilio school, I have a working knowledge of creating an Atelier space within the classroom. I have a passion for not only inspiring children to be lifelong learners but modeling it as well.

I commit to be a teacher who offers your children not only a vibrant education but an opportunity to build confidence and become independent individuals who are mindful of the world around them and interested in learning and growing into the peacemakers and change agents the world needs.

Robin Norgren, M.A.
M.A. Theology, Fuller Theological Seminary
B.S. Management, Arizona State University
A.M.S. Primary Certification, KHT Montessori
A.M.I. Primary Certification Candidate, S.I.M.S.
Life Coaching Certification, S.W.I.H.A.

CLICK HERE to view my freebies

CLICK HERE to view my drawing lessons

CLICK HERE to view my Art with the Masters projects

CLICK HERE to view my Contemporary Artist lessons

CLICK HERE to view art lessons that go along with popular books

CLICK HERE to view my self-esteem projects

CLICK HERE to view my class mural ideas

CLICK HERE to view my fun art folk art lessons

CLICK HERE to view 3 Bundled Lessons

CLICK HERE to view 5 Bundled lessons

CLICK HERE to check my reviews

OR

ORDER DIRECTLY FROM ME!

http://www.brightchildmontessori.com

is where you will find all my lesson plans and supplemental materials to make your Montessori Experience an enjoyable one.

Made in the USA
Monee, IL
02 July 2023

38406267R00069